Abraham's Great Discovery

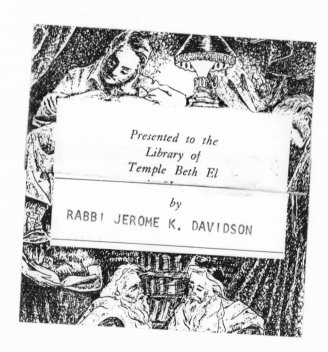

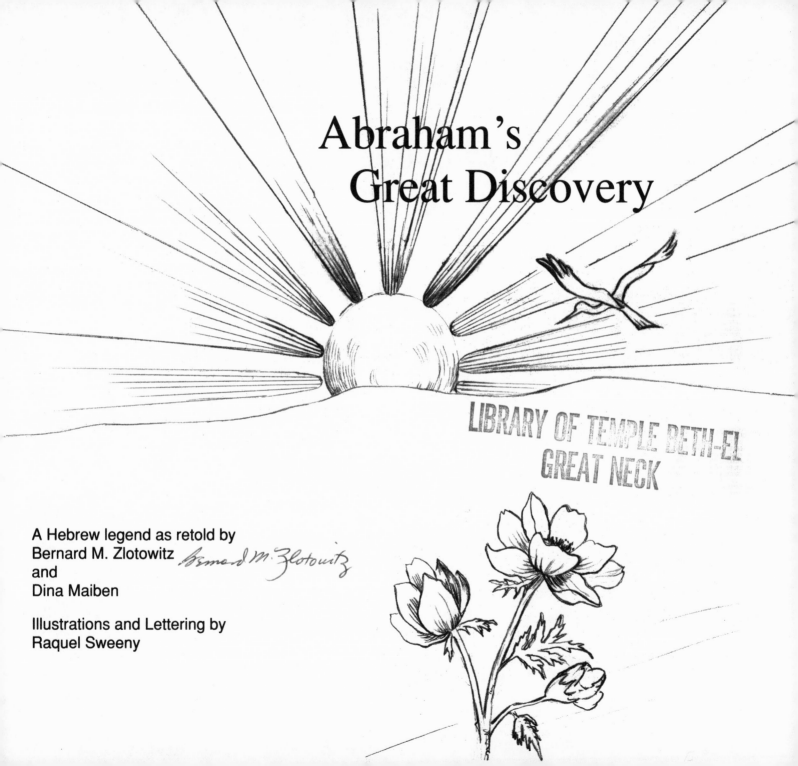

Abraham's Great Discovery

A Hebrew legend as retold by
Bernard M. Zlotowitz
and
Dina Maiben

Illustrations and Lettering by
Raquel Sweeny

Text copyright © 1991 by Bernard M. Zlotowitz and Dina Maiben
Illustrations copyright © 1991 by Raquel Sweeny

Library of Congress Catalog Card Number: 91-60474

Printed in the U.S.A.

First Printing 1991

ISBN 0-911389-04-0

Published in the United States by NightinGale Resources
Box 322
Cold Spring, New York 10516-0322

To my granddaughter, Marissa Greenberg,
who brings only joy and love.

Bernard M. Zlotowitz

For Jessica Nappa-Siegel and David Davis
"Happy is the one who seeks wisdom".

Dina Maiben

To Mariele and Rosilene, who are part of this book.

R.S.

Abraham was a little boy who lived many years ago in the far-away kingdom of Ur. Abraham's father was called Terah. His mother's name we do not know, and Nahor and Haran were the names of Abraham's brothers. They all loved one another very much.

Like all little boys, Abraham and his brothers loved to play. Sometimes they played in the big, beautiful garden next to their house. Sometimes they chased each other through the crowded streets. But their favorite place to play was in their father's workshop.

Abraham's father had a large workshop where he made and sold statues. He had some very, very big statues, some smaller ones and some tiny ones.

People bought a statue because they thought that the statue was a god. The people would bring the statue home and pray to it.

Now Abraham was like all the people at that time. He also believed that statues were gods. As he began to grow up, he started to ask:

"Is a statue really god?
It can't hear and it can't see.
It can't talk and it can't walk.
It is just wood, or clay, or stone.
It is just dumb!"

But his father, and his mother, and his brothers told him that it was a god, and he believed them.

As time went on, it bothered Abraham more and more:
"Is a statue really a god?" Everyone told him it was, but Abraham no longer believed them. He said,
"It can't be a god. It is just a piece of wood, and I'm going to prove it!"

He waited and waited, and one day he got
the chance to prove it. His father, Terah,
had to go away and he told Abraham
to mind the shop while he was gone.
After his father left, Abraham walked
around and around the shop, carefully
inspecting all of the statues. He stopped
in front of a big statue. Abraham said
to the statue:

"Statue, statue near the wall, talk!"
But the statue didn't talk.
For how could a statue talk?
It has a mouth but cannot talk.

Abraham said to himself, "Well, it can't talk, perhaps it can walk." Abraham spoke to the big statue again.

"Statue, statue near the wall, walk!"
But the statue didn't walk.
For how could a statue walk?
It has two feet but cannot walk.

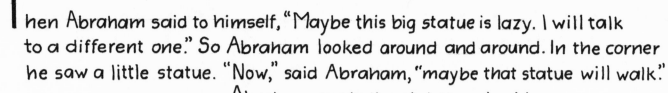

Then Abraham said to himself, "Maybe this big statue is lazy. I will talk to a different one." So Abraham looked around and around. In the corner he saw a little statue. "Now," said Abraham, "maybe that statue will walk." Abraham ran to the statue and said:

"Little statue, little statue,
Standing in the corner,
Little statue, little statue,
Please obey this order: walk!"
But the statue didn't walk.
For how could a statue walk?
It has two feet but cannot walk.

braham said to himself, "Maybe it's so small that it hasn't learned to walk. I'll ask the little statue it's name. I'm sure it could tell me that." Abraham turned to the little statue again and said:

"Little statue, little statue,
Standing in the corner,
Little statue, little statue,
Please obey this order:
Tell me your name!"
But the statue didn't talk.
For how could a statue talk?
It has a mouth but cannot talk.

Abraham turned to all the statues in the shop and said:

"You are no gods.
You can't walk.
And you can't talk.
You can't do anything!
You are just made of wood, or clay, or stone.
You are just statues!
I'm not praying to you anymore!"

Then Abraham took a club and smashed
all the statues in his father's workshop.
But the biggest statue he did not harm.
He placed the club in the big statue's hands
and waited for his father to return.

When his father, Terah, came back that afternoon, he couldn't believe his eyes. His broken statues were scattered all over the workshop.

"Abraham!" Terah shouted. "Where are you?"

"Here father," Abraham answered from his hiding place under the worktable. "Is something wrong?"
"Just look at this place," cried his father.
"Abraham! What did you do?"

"Father," Abraham said, "the big statue got angry with all the other statues and beat them up. Look! It is still holding the club!"

Terah's face got redder and redder. He clenched his fists and grit his teeth in anger and shouted,

"Impossible! Statues can't beat each other up! They are just made of wood, or clay, or stone. They can't do anything!"

"So why do you pray to them?" Abraham asked. "If they can't do anything how could they be gods?" Terah had no answer. He stood stone silent.

Then Abraham knew that statues are not gods,
and he wasn't going to pray to them ever again.
"I want to pray to God," Abraham thought
to himself. "But where is God and who is God?"

One afternoon after school, Abraham took a long walk through
the city of Ur. He walked and walked. Suddenly he stopped.
"Maybe the sun shining above is God," he said to himself.
"The sun makes everyone happy. It makes the waters warm
so we can swim. It shines all day so we can romp
and play." Abraham said:

"O sun, you must be God!
I'll pray to you!"

So Abraham prayed to the sun.

But when the night came, there was no sun. It had just disappeared.
Abraham said:

"O sun, you can't be God,
Here today and gone tonight."

Then he saw the moon above, and oh, how happy he was. He said:

"O moon, how beautiful you are!
You give light and you are bright.
You must be God. I'll pray to you!"

When morning came, the moon was gone
and the sun was back again. And
Abraham said:
"O moon, here tonight
and gone tomorrow,
You can't be God!
For God is always here!
God never disappears!"
Abraham cried and cried, because
he couldn't pray to God. He didn't
know where God is or who God is.

On another day Abraham took a walk throug[h]
the fields, and as he walked and walked,
He saw the sun shining
and the animals playing
The trees budding and
the flowers blossoming.
He heard the birds singing and
the lions roaring,
The donkeys braying and
the cows lowing.

The whole world was beautiful and at peace. And suddenly
Abraham understood. "I know who God is! God made this
whole world and watches over it!" He said:

"God made the heavens above and the earth beneath.
God made the sun to shine and the moon to glow.
God made the stars to twinkle and the trees to bud.
God made the birds to sing and the lions to roar.
God made you and me. God made everything.

"And I know where God is!" He said:

"God is in heaven and God is on earth.
God is all over this world of ours.
We can't see God, but God can see us.
God is the love we know and the warmth we feel.
God is the kindness and the sweetness we enjoy.
This is God, there is none else!"

And so it was that Abraham learned about the one true God, the only God, who made the heavens above and the earth beneath, and everything for you and me.

Abraham ran and jumped with joy,
clapping his hands and shouting
God's praises all the way home.

		DATE DUE	